PROPHETIC WORDS

FOR
PROPHETIC PEOPLE

*Prophetic words of hope,
help, and encouragement for every
season of your year*

MALACHI TALABI

Author, public and itinerant speaker

"Lord, whatever you're doing in this season, don't do it without me."

Those are famous song lyrics by Bishop Paul Morton. But think about them, what if God was up to something, wouldn't you like to know it? Imagine being on the same wavelength as God? Some people have a knack for predicting things that are going to happen; they are futurists who can see trends and predict events. Until I was born again, I couldn't predict things I didn't really notice any patterns or themes in my life or the seasons that I was going through. But there are patterns and seasons in life ; Suddenly the Holy Spirit began to show me things to come. I started to become more sensitive to His plans, and I started noticing things more intently. I believe this came about from spending time praying in tongues for extended periods, as well as spending time in stillness and journaling.

Things to come revealed

As I began to pick up on things to come (seasons of blessings, warfare or even what the pastor would be preaching about on Sunday) I couldn't ignore it. I didn't get these revelations from a prophet or YouTube messages. All I know is that occasionally, God would speak to me about what was going to happen in the month, and those things *would* happen. I am not talking about political events or economic events but, rather, the things that God was going to do for His people.

If God told me (while journaling) that it was a time of abundance, not only would unexpected finances come into my life and the lives of other people around me, but what excited me is that trusted prophets or people with the gift of prophecy would be saying the very same thing.

I want to stress that it wasn't an overnight thing this happened over a period of years. I wouldn't ask God what was happening in the month or year, but I would journal, read the Bible, or pray, and I'd pick up a theme for the month, the next six months or even the year.

I remember a time when God shared a word with me; I sent it to my mentor, Mark Virkler, to check if he thought it was God speaking to me, to my surprise he asked if he could share it with his network of people that's thousands of people!. I was shocked. After that I knew the message wasn't just for me, so I shared it on social media with a small group of people I pray with. I was blown away when people sent me pictures and messages telling me that prophets and ministries they knew had said the exact same thing that I had said on the very same day.

An example would be a word God gave me recently about a shower of blessing coming. I shared it with the words below:

"God is going to pour out a shower of blessing this April; you'll be dripping with blessings, so get ready." (See **Ezekiel 34:26**).

A day later, I saw that prophetess **Cindy Jacobs** had put the following message on her social media account:

"I just decree over you showers of blessing. I decree over you the power of God visiting your body, raising you up where you have been fighting infirmities. I tell the infirmities to go! I send showers of healing, showers of joy, showers of blessing upon you right now in the name of Jesus!" **Ezekiel 34:26**

Love you guys and God bless you!

Cindy Jacobs

This has happened so many times across the years that I had to pay attention to it. I realised that God wants us to know the times and seasons; it's to our advantage.

Knowing the times and seasons

"The sons of Issachar who had understanding of the times, to know what Israel ought to do, their chiefs were two hundred; and all their brethren were at their command;"

There was a prophetic tribe in Israel, called the sons of Issachar, that knew the times, and this knowledge helped Israel make decisions regarding war and welfare. Imagine having divine insight into what will happen in the future and what's on God's agenda. This is priceless, and it's possible. The Bible tells us the Holy Spirit will show us things to come.

In the Book of Genesis, Joseph predicted a time of famine and a time of fortune, and with this insight, he knew what to do over a fourteen year period. Imagine knowing what to do financially for the next fourteen years. I am not saying I know all these things, but I do know that God has given me glimpses into particular seasons, and this has bought me hope, help, and encouragement.

God has a plan

God has a plan and a blueprint, and it's to our advantage to know the plans God has for us so that we can partner with them. As I've grown, I've heard God speak to me about a month, a three-month period, a six-month period, and even a year.

What I began to notice is that the same things would happen in similar periods of the year. For instance, if March was a time of healing one year, it would be similar for the next year. I noticed there were certain *windows* of blessings and breakthroughs in the year, and when I picked up these patterns, I started to live with expectation and confidence because I knew a season of blessing was coming.

I remember looking back at my journal over a two-year period and noticing that every April, God would do miraculous things for my family financially. My phone would start ringing, and I'd be invited to a speaking engagement or asked to lead a coaching session. I began to see April as **a set time of blessings.**

God works in seasons, not just months

When writing this book, I thought it would be nice to give a word for each month, but that's not what God has given me. God gives me seasonal words—sometimes he speaks to me about a particular month and sometimes he gives me multiple words for the same season. Some months are themed in this book and some seasons have multiple words. God is not rigid, and I can give you only what He has given me.

This book is written in seasons from December to February, March to May, June to August, and September to November. The writing isn't designed to govern your decision-making but to show you what to expect in the seasons of your year. As you read, pray and journal and ask God to direct you. But just know that throughout your year, God has a plan and there are seasons that the manifestation of his goodness is heightened.

All prophecies in this book – in fact, all prophecies that you receive – should be carefully tested, weighed, and considered prayerfully. If the words resonate with you, pray then believe God for their manifestation.

1 Thessalonians 5:20-21

Contents Page

INTRODUCTION

A Prophetic Perspective on God's Promises

> *"For I know the plans I have for you," declares the LORD, "plans to prosper you and not to harm you, plans to give you hope and a future."*
> **(Jeremiah 29:11)**

If you have a promise, prophecy, or personal dream from God and you feel like it's moving in slow motion, don't worry at all. Just because your promise hasn't arrived yet doesn't mean it's not on its way. During the early parts of the year, people often lose hope because they think God's promise manifests instantly. I tell you for a fact that it rarely does.

Here are five little-known facts about your promises, prophecies, and personal dreams. Most people don't know these truths and spend their lives angry, frustrated, and confused. When you understand these truths, you may speed up the arrival of your promise, and at the very least, you'll have a broader understanding of the science of God's promises. This will help you make sense of the madness and release you from any frustration you may feel in the meantime.

1) YOUR PROMISED LAND IS OUTSIDE YOUR COMFORT ZONE

When God makes you a promise, it will always require you to step outside of your comfort zone—out of the place where things are familiar; out of your usual routine. God showed up in Abraham's life and said "Abraham, I have some promises for you, but they are all outside of your comfort zone. Go from your country, your people, and your father's house to a land that I will show you." (Genesis 12:1) While God didn't give him the details, He gave him the direction, and the direction was to move outside of his comfort zone. Abraham had been too comfortable to receive God's promise.

When God wants to do something unusual, He will separate you from the familiar.

Before you can step into your zone of greatness, you must first step out of your zone of comfort. Your promised land will always be outside of this comfort zone.

2) YOUR PROPHECIES ARE DEPENDENT ON KAIROS, NOT ROLEX

When you get a prophetic word, there is a huge temptation to put a time limit on it. Your mind starts doing calculations and estimations. This is very dangerous because there are two time zones in the universe. There is Rolex time, which is the chronological time we live by every day, such as 7 pm, 2 weeks, or 6 months. Then there is *kairos* time, which has nothing to do with numbers or digits and everything to do with divine seasons. When it comes to your prophecies, if you live by Rolex time you'll be discouraged because your prophecies are always dependent on *kairos* time. Your vision is for an appointed time (Habakkuk 2:3); not Rolex time, not your time, but *kairos* time. Your age shouldn't be a factor. How many years you've waited shouldn't be a factor because you don't live by Rolex time, you live by *kairos* time.

3) YOUR PROMISE WILL HAVE PRESSURE AND PLEASURE ATTACHED TO IT

If you know anything about the promised land that God gave the children of Israel, you'll see that the people who went to spy on the land discovered that it was flowing with milk and honey but it was also inhabited by giants and other dangerous tribes. This was the promised land God gave to his people! Your ideal promise would probably be milk and honey alone, but God attaches pressure and pleasure to every promise He gives you because He knows that pressure and pleasure are the two forces that bring out the best in you. They are the two great human motivators for creation and productivity. Marriage is full of pressure and pleasure. Business is full of pressure and pleasure. Giving birth to a child is full of pressure and pleasure. (Just ask any woman who's given birth!) If you think it's going to be all milk and honey, you are in for a shock.

God doesn't want your promised land to make you a spiritual slouch.

The giants represent pressure and the milk and honey represent *pleasure*. Your promise will have these two elements attached to it.

4) AFTER RECEIVING A PROPHETIC WORD, YOU MUST MOVE FROM CELEBRATION TO PARTICIPATION

I remember receiving a prophetic word and speaking about it for weeks and weeks. I would say to my wife, "Mildred, can you believe what the prophet said to me?!" I phoned some friends and retold the story again and again. I was in celebration mode. Sometimes the awesomeness of the supernatural can get you too excited. I was still celebrating my prophecy months later when I noticed it hadn't come to pass. I realised that celebration wouldn't make my prophecy come to pass—participation would! Most prophecies come with a part for you to play, whether that is *explicit* or *implicit*. Abraham needed to be intimate with his wife; that was his participation. The children of Israel had to cross the Red Sea—that was *their* participation.

If God said you are going to the Olympics, you'd better find yourself in the gym! If He says you are a worship leader, then for the sake of your audience, get vocal lessons!

Making the shift from celebration to participation will accelerate the manifestation of your prophetic word.

So, when you get a prophetic word, always ask yourself, "What is my part?"

5) YOU MUST BE PROCESSED BEFORE YOUR PROMISE IS MADE MANIFEST

Ok, here's the BIG one...

The big print is the promise; the small print is the process.

God is loud about the promise but quiet about the process. God knows if you saw the process, you wouldn't want the promise. Check it out—He told David that he would be King but didn't tell him anything about the giants. He told Jeremiah that he would be a prophet but didn't tell him he was going to jail. He showed Joseph he'd be a leader but he didn't tell him about the pit. There is a process attached to your promise. Don't run from it, embrace it.

Partnering with the Prophetic

1. Understand there is a process to God's promise

2. Create a vision board containing pictures of God's promises and pray over the vision board

3. Ask God what your part is in the manifestation of your promise

SECTION 1

Words for

December – February

"There is a time for everything, and a season for every activity under the heavens"

(Ecclesiastes 3:1)

CHAPTER 01

A DECEMBER TO REMEMBER

A time for God to do
unforgettable things
(Ezekiel 32:1, Psalms 65:11)

"This has been a tough year, but God kept me." That's what you'll hear in most Pentecostal churches at the end of the year. That's what I heard at almost every testimony service. It's easy to remember the struggles that you've been through, and by the end of the year most people (if they are honest) are just surviving, so the end of the year feels like the end of a very long, tiring race. That is not God's plan!

The end of a thing

*The end of a thing is meant to be **better** than the beginning (Ecclesiastes 7:8).* There is meant to be joy and celebration that comes at the end of a year. You are meant to end the year on a high note and take that momentum into the new year. After reading and receiving this month's prophetic word, you will look forward to every December because you'll start to see God outshine Himself and show up in ways that you could never remember before. God likes to show up with a BIG bang!

The prophetic word

I remember reading my Bible and turning to Ezekiel 32:1. I don't know why, but I just turned there and I was shocked. Here's what the verse says:

"And it came to pass in the twelfth year, in the twelfth month, in the first day of the month, that the word of the Lord came unto me, saying,"

What shocked me is that scripture mentions **the first day of the twelfth month.** I happened to be reading the scripture on the **first of December.** The timing had to be God's! It felt like God walked into my bedroom as if He had a message just for me. I was on edge, anticipating what He would say, and I was led to Psalms 65:11.

"Thou crownest the year with thy goodness; and thy paths drop fatness"

This verse says that God crowns the year with goodness. I love the way the Holy Spirit speaks and leads. I put both scriptures together and this is what I got:

"In the twelfth month on the first day, the word of the LORD came to me saying, Thou crownest the year with thy goodness; and thy paths drop fatness."

This is amazing! To think that God would crown the year, that means that every month His hand will be with you! A crown is circular, and that can represent the whole year. God won't just crown your month, but He will crown your year. If you look closely at the verse, there is a promise of abundance and prosperity. Whenever you see the word "fat," I want you to think about finances, abundance, and provision. The scripture says your paths shall drip with fatness! God is going to do financial miracles and pour out a financial blessing this December! When this word came to me, I felt as if God were saying:

"Son, I am not finished. This December will be a December to remember. I've crowned your year with Goodness, and I will end your year with Goodness. Expect good things to happen this month, for this will be a December to remember."

This December, live with anticipation

A December I couldn't forget

Sometimes God gives last-minute blessings. I remember how at 11:45 pm on December the 31st one particular year my phone gave me an alert that someone bought an online course. I got excited because this was right at the very end of December and it was the first course I sold. God knew that I wouldn't forget this, and it was a fulfilment of His December-to-Remember word. I had received a financial blessings and a prophetic confirmation

This December, God will do something that you will remember. It may be healing, an answered prayer, an encounter, or a reconciliation. Lift up your faith and start to declare that this will be a December to remember.

Partnering with the Prophetic

1. Post on your social media that this will be a December to remember

2. Pray and personalise Psalms 65:11 continually

3. Ask God to do something that you will remember

4. Tell someone that this will be a December to remember

5. Journal what happens this December so that you can testify

CHAPTER 02

JANUARY

Your Month of Unexpected Harvest

Get ready to experience
an early harvest
Joel 2:23

What if you could experience the blessing of God without strain or struggle? What if you started the year full of fire and victory? How would you feel if this January was like no other and God sent you an unexpected blessing? January is usually a month when you kickstart a goal or a habit. You usually aren't expecting a harvest because you haven't spent much time yet sowing a seed. January is a month of energy and enthusiasm; a month when you can start fresh and do something new. But *prophetically*, January is much more than that.

The unexpected harvest

Once I was studying the rains of God. To be honest, I don't know why but I remember this was in January. I discovered that there were different seasons when it would rain in Israel; there was a rain called the *former rain* and another called the *latter rain*.

In Israel, rain is a blessing. Rain is needed for the successful growing and harvesting of crops. There are two rainy seasons mentioned in Scripture: the former rain, which is the autumn rain (October to November), and the latter, spring rain (March to April). With the former rain, farmers begin ploughing and planting seeds. Then the latter rain, which is even more important, matures the crops for the harvest.

Rain is a blessing for the land. Spiritually and prophetically, rain is a blessing! When God said He would open up the windows of heaven and pour out a blessing, He gives us a picture of sufficient rain on the land to help produce a harvest.

While studying, I read Joel 2:23 and saw a promise that leaped off the page. It felt mystical because of the specific time I had been reading this scripture. Dates and times are important to God, and He often reveals things to you at *specific times* to get your attention. Here's the scripture:

"Be glad then, ye children of Zion, and rejoice in the Lord your God: for he hath given you the former rain moderately, and he will cause to come down for you the rain, the former rain, and the latter **rain in the first month.**"

A time for unexpected blessings

God promised to provide everything that was needed for seeding time and harvest in the first month! Yes, He said everything needed to reap a harvest. Think about it. Usually, you would have to wait for the rain to soften the ground, plant your seed, and then wait for the rain that brings in the harvest. This can take many months! But in His promise, God said in the first month He would pour out both rains.

This is God bypassing the natural process of things and bringing an unexpected blessing and an acceleration of manifestation! When I received this promise I was reading it in the first month of *my year* and God had taken this scripture and made it real for me. My expectation rose as you read the scripture let your faith rise.

God will pour out the latter rain and the former rain for you *this month* in January. As you read this, I want you to believe that blessings are coming this month, and you're not going to have to toil, strain, or work extra hard.

For me, that January God provided a financial blessing. I received a higher-than-expected financial turnover in one of my businesses. I couldn't believe it. Since then, I have always declared that God will pour out the latter rain and the former rain in the first month. I want you to know that God can pour more of his spirit, His anointing, and His presence this month. The blessing isn't restricted to finances. The important thing is to understand that God wants to give you an unexpected harvest. He wants to surprise you with His blessings, and He wants you to start the year as you mean to go on, which is from Glory to Glory.

This is the month expect an unexpected blessing!

Partnering with the Prophetic

1. Declare this as your month of unexpected blessings
2. Pray this prayer

"Lord, You said You will send the latter rain and the former rain in the first month. Send the rain. Send Your unexpected blessings, accelerate my harvest, and let me know that it is Your hand at work. Thank You in advance. Amen."

December – February –
Read- *Ezekiel 32:1,*
Psalms 65:11 Joel 2:23)

Confessions for this season

1. *God will do unforgettable things in my life*

2. *I will experience an early harvest*

END-OF-SEASON TESTIMONY

What did God do for you in this season?

....

....

....

....

....

....

....

....

....

....

....

....

....

....

....

....

....

....

....

END-OF-SEASON TESTIMONY

What blessings or breakthroughs did you experience?

....

....

....

....

....

....

....

....

....

....

....

....

....

....

....

....

....

....

SECTION
2

Words for

March - May

CHAPTER 03

THIS SPRING IS YOUR SPRING

– *A season of transformation and revelation begins*

(Isaiah 43:19)

A song came into my heart as I stood in a shopping line waiting for medicine for my kids:

> *It's a new season, it's a new day*
> *A fresh anointing is flowing my way*
> *It's a season of power and prosperity*
> *It's a new season coming to me*

This is an Israel Houghton song, and I realised it was God singing over me (see Zephaniah 3:17) God can do that sometimes. What I mean by singing over me is highlighting a particular song so it's stuck in your head or drawing your attention to a song. But why? Why this song?

It wasn't until I got into the secret place that I received a download of revelation. God asked me, "Son, what season is it?" I googled the season and discovered spring was about to start. This was the day before—the first of March.

Then while journaling the Lord said:

I am doing a new thing. It's a new season.

> *Behold, I will do a new thing; now it shall **spring forth**; shall ye not know it? I will even make a way in the wilderness, and rivers in the desert.*
> *(Isaiah 43:19)*

I want you to notice that I will do a new thing. This time I want you to behold it. For a long time, you've been striving and pushing, but in this season, you will behold Me doing new things in your life.

This spring will be your spring.

Just like jumping on a trampoline—you always move to different heights. So shall it be this spring, when you experience elevation. You will go higher and have more joy, and as you go higher and higher into a new season and a new level, I shall cause you to flourish, to reap, and to have a harvest—a plentiful harvest. Everything associated with spring is yours THIS spring.

I felt God say to me that four things will happen in spring, from the first of March to the thirty-first of May:

1. THERE WILL BE A SPRING IN YOUR STEP (Transportation)

2. THINGS WILL SPRING TO MIND (Revelation)

3. GOD WILL DO SOME SPRING CLEANING (Sanctification)

4. YOUR HEALTH SHALL SPRING FORTH (Rejuvenation)

1) THERE WILL BE A SPRING IN YOUR STEP

According to the Oxford dictionary:

"If you walk with or **have a spring in your step,** *you walk energetically in a way that shows you are feeling happy and confident."*

Expect new energy, vitality, and spiritual refreshing. Depression will be far from you, oppression will be far from you, and you'll have new levels of energy—a new thirst for life. The joy of the Lord will be your strength, and people will notice the spring in your step.

2) THINGS WILL SPRING TO MIND

According to the Oxford dictionary, the term "spring to mind" means:

"(of a thought or idea) to suddenly occur to someone."

In this season, you will receive an influx of words of knowledge—what I and my wife call "WoW moments" (Words of Wisdom moments). Spontaneous thoughts, ideas, eureka moments, aha moments, hunches, intuition – all really the voice of the Holy Spirit – will increase in this season; at work, during play, in prayer, wherever you are. So, take a notepad with you, expecting things to spring to mind.

3) GOD WILL DO SOME SPRING CLEANING

In Jewish custom, spring cleaning is linked to Passover in March or April, which marks the liberation of Jews from slavery in Egypt. Before the start of the holiday, a general cleaning takes place in order to remove any yeast bread, or chametz, from the home.

Your body is the temple of the Holy Spirit. Every now and then the Holy Spirit wants to do some spring cleaning. Maybe there's anger in the temple; He'll sweep that away. Maybe there's bitterness; He'll clean that away. Maybe there's unforgiveness; expect God to deal with all the rats in the attic and clean the temple so that you can have a clearer channel to hear His voice and to fulfil your calling. Also, expect Him to clean your motives, your inner circle, and even your physical diet—all things that may hinder you from living the life he created you to live.

4) YOUR HEALING SHALL SPRING FORTH SPEEDILY – REJUVENATION

Isaiah 58:8 speaks of healing springing forth. And in this season, as we lean in and listen to the Lord, we will experience rejuvenation—a new burst of health. This won't just happen supernaturally, but wisdom will come concerning diet and exercise; a passion and desire to get fit and eat right will come just in time for summer!

Break out of the box

The jack-in-the-box was an image God gave me. He said the jack works with a spring. This season you will break out of the boxes you've had and the boxes people have put you in.

This spring will be your spring. Behold the work of the Lord in the next three months.

Partnering with the Prophetic

1. Declare that this spring is your spring

2. Ask God what He wants to do for you in this season (sanctification, transformation, revelation, or rejuvenation)

3. Read through these words a few more times this week to remind yourself about the blessing of this season

CHAPTER 04

PROJECT BUTTERFLY

– *Your Season to Fly*

On the 21st of March, I was walking in my garden and saw a flower that I hadn't planted. The flower was purple and it was beautiful. As I wondered what it was, the thought came, "What is happening in your garden is happening in your life."

But I dismissed it.

Later that day, I was teaching an online group on the value of speaking in tongues and suddenly the word "tulip" flew into my mind.

I realised that it was spring season, and Spring is tulip season. The flower in my garden was a tulip and God was trying to get my attention.So, I went to the Lord in prayer and asked, "Lord, is there anything You want to say to me in this season?" Here is what I picked up:

"Spring is the time of new life—the time for the butterfly to emerge, the time for the cocoon to hatch, the time when the things that I promised will be made manifest. The winter has passed, and now it's time for those things and those skills and those talents that were hidden to be revealed, to come out, to spring forth.

This is a great time to birth things. This is a great time to start new things as there is newness in the atmosphere. The tulip is significant, as it demonstrates newness.

You noticed the tulip because I wanted you to discern that you are in a new season. In this season, lots of things are going to happen – success, fun, joy – this is a GREAT season! It's a season when you see much happiness and breakthrough.

There is a time for everything, and THIS is a time for success."

This is your season

In the evening, I was watching Peacemaker, an action-adventure program, and the team leader said to the hero:

"I have a project for you; it's called Project Butterfly"!

The Holy Spirit reminded me that eight hours earlier, God was talking to me about the butterfly's journey, so I knew God was bringing confirmation.

Butterflies – THIS IS YOUR SEASON!

I know that in this season you are going to fly to new heights, for it's time to come out of the cocoon and come out of hiding. Imposter syndrome will be no more because the butterfly is about to soar.

This season will be a season when you are going to be positioned in places that God has been preparing you for, and all the pain and pressure of the past will now make sense because it was all preparation and transformation for this new season and position.

This will be your season to walk in the pre-ordained plan of God, and previous pain will turn into purpose. What ever new things God has put on your heart move towards them with confidence that they manifest will and your will soar.

Partnering with the Prophetic

1. Write down something new you want to do (write a book, start a business, or new job)

2. Pray for promotion and success as you move toward your goal (do this daily)

CHAPTER 05

APRIL SHOWERS

The blessings of God will be poured out like never before

Ezekiel 34:26

On the first of April, I heard the words "April showers." Yep—"April showers." This was a spontaneous thought that ran through my mind, and then I heard the phrase "latter rain."

I went to my Bible and found this scripture….

> *"I will make them and the places surrounding my*

hill a blessing. I will
send down showers in
season; there will be
showers of blessing."
Ezekiel 34:26

The promise

I believe God is going to pour an immense blessing on His people. There is a shower coming, and this is NOT a normal shower. This is a *shower of blessings. Here's what I journaled:*

"Many have forgotten that I am a supernatural God.

I do cancel debts.

I do heal cancer.

I do open blind eyes; I do deliver.

I am not powerless. I am powerful. I am the I AM, I am.

You shall see My supernatural hand in this season.

I am that God, and I will shower down blessings on My people. This is what I am doing in this season. This is My Agenda.

There is an April shower of blessings coming.

The latter rain is coming. Expect a blessing; expect big things to happen. This is a time when I will pour out. There is a blessing, a shower coming, and nothing can stop this supply of blessing to the people of God..

The ground has been prepared; it shall rain this time. The latter rain shall not fail.

April showers, April showers, April showers. Yes, there will be April showers; you will have a shower of blessings.

Blessings will just pop up out of nowhere—blessing upon blessing, shower after shower after shower. You are entering a season of blessing; a time of blessing—a time when you'll see My hand supernaturally. And for those who have planted, I am going to rain on the land. I am going to rain on the things you have planted.

It will rain. No famine, no doubt, no drought. No famine— you shall see the rain. The latter rain is here."

Joel 2

*Be glad, people of Zion, rejoice in the LORD your God, for He has given you the autumn rains because He is faithful. He sends you abundant showers, both autumn and **spring rains,** as before. The threshing floors will be filled with grain; the vats will overflow with **new wine and oil. I will repay you** for the years the locusts have eaten – the great locust and the young locust, the other locusts, and the locust swarm – My great army that I sent among you. **You will have plenty to eat until you are full,** and you will praise the name of the LORD your God, **who has worked wonders for you; never again will My people be shamed.***

You are about to enter a season of unprecedented blessings.

- Opportunities

- Payback

- Growth

- Open doors

- Breakthrough

- Abundance

- Prosperity

Insight

Flow, you shall flow with My spirit. You shall experience Me more than ever before. Blessing upon blessings; I'm not finished yet. I have revealed My agenda for this season, so watch and see."

I pray the Lord rains on you, your family, and your ministry in this season. It's important to document any blessings are answered prayers that you receive in this period for they will be fuel for your faith for the rest of the year

Partnering with the Prophetic

1. Expect God to shower down his blessings

2. Journal every blessing this month

3. Testify on the phone, in church, or to a friend about the many blessings you experience

March – May

Confessions for this season

1. *This spring is my Spring!*

2. *I will experience an April shower of blessings*

Ezekiel 34:26 (Isaiah 43:19)

49

END-OF-SEASON TESTIMONY

What did God do for you in this season?

....

....

....

....

....

....

....

....

....

....

....

....

....

....

....

....

....

END-OF-SEASON TESTIMONY

What blessings or breakthroughs did you experience?

....

....

....

....

....

....

....

....

....

....

....

....

....

....

....

....

....

SECTION
3

Words for

June
– August

CHAPTER 06

THE NEXT SIX MONTHS WILL BE YOUR BEST SIX MONTHS

Be prepared! God will
outdo Himself
Job 42:10-12

Your Job 42:10-12 Your moment

*T*he next months will be your best six months. This is going to be a season of manifestation, you are going to see the things you have been imagining. Your dreams and the things on your vision board are going to appear.

This is your time, your season, and your moment. God is going to do big, big things according to your faith. This is a season for the manifestation of a double portion. What God did for Job He will do for you.

"So the Lord blessed the latter end of Job more than his beginning: for he had fourteen thousand sheep, and six thousand camels, and a thousand yoke of oxen, and a thousand she asses."

It's important to see yourself in scripture, and every now and again when you do, God begins to make His word come alive. It's as if you feel God is speaking directly to you; that's what prophecy is—God speaking to you! Here is how I saw the scripture as I was reading it:

"And the lord blessed the latter half of Malachi's year more than He did the beginning of his year."

I want you to write out the sentence above; insert your name and read it out loud. Can you feel the anointing from that? I want you to think about it. You've been blessed from December to February (in the autumn season) because God poured out the latter and former rain in the first month. And you've had a December to remember, and you've been blessed in Spring because this Spring was your Spring, and God was doing amazing work as you flew to new heights in various areas of your life.

Now, with all the blessings that you've experienced so far, God is **saying the next six months will be your best six months!** He's going to outdo himself, outshine himself, and perform more than you can ask for or imagine. That's something to get excited about.

When I first received this word, I didn't know what to expect until I realised it's totally biblical to expect to go from *Glory to Glory!* Live in expectation! Expect God to do bigger things, expect more blessings, and mix these words with your faith!

One of the things God made me do at the halfway point of the year was to re-vision; that is, to rewrite my vision, look at all the goals that I had at the beginning of the year, and rewrite them.

You tick off the ones that have been achieved and pray about the ones that still need to be made manifest. This is an important step. So don't read on; do it now. As you do, you'll get more revelation and clarity, and this will give you all the fire and inspiration you need to play your part in the things God wants to do—for you and through you.

Remember, the next six months will be your best six months! And the next six months will be a blessed six months. God is going to make the last half of the year better than the first half of the year.

Partnering with the Prophetic

1. Confess that the next six months are going to be a blessed six months

2. Rewrite your vision and pray into it

3. Celebrate the things God has already done and expect even more

CHAPTER 07

YOUR SEASON FOR A DOUBLE PORTION

Elshaddi is going to show up and bless you with double

Isaiah 61:7

*And **these signs shall follow them** that believe.*

Prophetic signs of a coming blessing

Have you ever had a natural sign reveal a divine promise? You know things like seeing things on billboards, hearing songs that contain phrases linked to things you've prayed about, strange little God winks kept happening to me. I felt like God was using all He could use to communicate the approaching season of blessing.

God did something special. He has a special way of confirming His word, and with me, it's usually something funny.

I was ordering food at a McDonald's drive-through with my kids; as I picked up my order and began to drive home, a man on a motorbike waved at me to pull over. I was going to ignore him, but he was persistent. I thought I had a flat tire or that there was something wrong with my car lights, so I wound down my window.

He said, "Mate, I'm a delivery driver at McDonald's. A customer has cancelled his order and I'm giving it all to you!.... but I'm taking the drinks." He smiled, gave me the huge bag, and drove off.

So, I left with my original order and another big, FREE bag of McDonald's. I turned to my kids and said, "Girls, God just blessed us!" I mean, it could have been anybody driving through at that time, but it was ME! I was in the right place at the right time.

I didn't just take the food and good home and eat it. I journaled as soon as I got home. I have learned that when things like this happen, there's usually a message from heaven encoded in the circumstance. This isn't always the case, but on this occasion it was. Sometimes you can read too much into circumstances and step into presumption, which is dangerous. But when God is speaking through circumstances, He usually brings confirmation.

When I journaled, I felt the Holy Spirit say, *"Malachi, you almost missed the real revelation in the McDonald's visitation; it wasn't just about Me blessing you, it was about Me giving you a DOUBLE PORTION!*

I got excited and even posted the picture and the journal on social media. It was good that I did because two weeks later my wife came home and said, "Malachi, look inside this bag. I was at a McDonald's (not the same one as I went to) and when I got my order I received TWO Big macs rather than just one." Then, a week after that, my wife packed lunch for my children and bought them a particular sweet. Their school teacher rewarded them with two sweets for good work and the sweets she gave our children were the very same size, brand, and flavour as the one my wife packed earlier in the morning. So, we all received a, literally, double portion. God was clearly speaking.

This is going to be a season of breakthrough and anointing. Double is coming.

The prophetic word

*"Double was in your spirit but now it will be in your natural. This is going to be a season of manifestation, so what will happen is that God is going to do big, big things according to your faith. This is a season for manifestation and of the **double portion**".*

I want to look at Isaiah 61: 7 specifically:

*Instead of your shame you will receive a **double portion**, and instead of disgrace you will rejoice in your inheritance. And so you will inherit a **double portion** in your land, and everlasting joy will be yours.*

It says for your shame you'll receive **double**.

God is going to give you double for your shame! He's going to vindicate you, and all the pain, shame, and defeat are going to be worth it! Nothing is going to be wasted, and if you are reading this, you know that this is God's agenda! I have seen this in my life so many times.

I remember leaving a workplace I had been working at for over a decade and getting little tribute and celebration. I worked extremely hard and was promoted by every manager but when I left my manager felt bitter (maybe because I was leaving and they wanted me to stay) her last speech during my last day was full of side jokes about me. It was dishonourable; I was upset.

A few months later, I found another job and worked there for five weeks; not only did I quickly build rapport but, the honour that I received when I left was unbelievable. I received cards, sweets, and prayers, and there were even tears. This was astonishing! I knew that God was giving me double honour. This has happened many times, where God will give me double for my shame. I know what He has done for me in this season, and He will do the same for you.

Partnering with the Prophetic

1. Declare the scripture verse Isaiah 61:5 every day June – August read Isaiah 61:5 Job 42:10-12

2. Say "The next six months will be my best six months"

Confessions for this season
This is my time for a double portion; I will receive double for my shame

END-OF-SEASON TESTIMONY

What did God do for you in this season?

....

....

....

....

....

....

....

....

....

....

....

....

....

....

....

....

....

....

....

....

END-OF-SEASON TESTIMONY

What blessings or breakthroughs did you experience?

....

....

....

....

....

....

....

....

....

....

....

....

....

....

....

....

....

SECTION
4

Words for
September
– November

CHAPTER 08

IT'S THE LAST QUARTER, A TIME TO PUSH!

Barrenness will be
broken in your life
Deuteronomy 7:14

"It's the last quarter; a time for you to push!"

I remember being chased by the number 444 I had been seeing licence plates with **4 4 4** on them, not knowing the meaning. This would happen everywhere, all the time. I just couldn't ignore it, so I started to take photos of the cars I would see for evidence, just in case God was speaking.

What was strange is that I didn't even know what 444 meant. I couldn't find a scripture for the numbers I was seeing, and I didn't pick up on anything which was very frustrating until, one day, I was still and asked God. I had done this before but I wasn't ready for God to speak my attitude was wrong I was moaning because I had no understanding rather than simply trusting that the answer would come at the right time. What was funny is that the answer wasn't anything that I could predict or would expect.

God drew my attention to the fact that September is the start of the **last quarter of the year.** It made the numbers I was seeing make sense. The numbers 444 were a reference to the number of **quarters that the year can be split into (given the twelve months of the year).**

The last quarter

God said, "This is the **last quarter,** *just like in a basketball game. Everything matters in this quarter, everything can turn around in this quarter, this quarter is the last chance to win the game, and this quarter is the time to bring on a hero, make that impossible shot, or do something that will completely guarantee victory."* Half-time is over; this is now the last quarter. It's time you go for every goal you haven't fulfilled. You need to be sprinting to the finish; you need to plan and refocus and push! You need to press toward the mark so that in December you can truly say, IT IS FINISHED and you can look back with Joy!"

God wants us to walk out of the year with VICTORY! But the last push starts now. If you are reading this **it's time for you to push!**

This is also a Sarah season

In the same season, while praying in tongues (which I believe is a great source of divine wisdom), the name "Sarah" popped out of my mouth in English. I went to the Bible and read up on Sarah.

Sarah was barren for a season but then she gave birth! The timing of this insight was perfect because I received this word in September and September is the ninth month. Nine months represents a time of birthing things that you have been carrying for a time; to push out what God has put in, and a time to manifest fruitfulness. Everything that is overdue shall now come forth.

Testimony from this season of birthing

On the first of September 2022, I received a contract for a **new job**. I also received an understanding of a situation I had been confused about for years. This is a season of birthing and breakthroughs! It's a season of fruitfulness and you shall no longer be barren.

71

CHAPTER 09

YOU ARE A FIRE STARTER

*You will burn with a passion, and
your fire will not go out*

Matthew 3:11

*I*t's bonfire night in the UK during November, but it's
also a great time to keep your spiritual fire burning.
*God loves fire. He spoke to Moses out of the burning bush;
we are also told He will fuel us with the Holy Spirit and
fire. Elijah called fire down from heaven. The examples
could go on forever. The main thing is to understand that,
spiritually, fire is a good thing.*

While praying, I saw a picture in my mind.

I saw a fireplace that got bigger, then started to burn a house, then the neighbourhood, then the city, then the globe.

I shared this vision at a Journaling with Jesus prophecy session that I run, telling the audience that we will carry fire wherever we go! A few days later, I was in a shopping centre, and the fire alarm went off. We were told to evacuate the shop. This happened on Thursday, the eighth of April 2021. A week or so later, I was sharing a Facebook message on LIVE, and as I was speaking, the fire alarm in my house went off. This was on the sixteenth of April, and it happened LIVE in front of many audience members."

What people don't know is that at crossover service back in 2017, I was speaking and, strangely enough, the fire alarm went off! That means that for the last few years, I have had three fire alarms go off during a speech.

The fire alarms that went off during this period confirmed the picture I had about the fireplace. It was something that God was giving me. Dramatic signs are designed; they aren't a game or a gimmick. They get our attention; knowing why God gives you signs and wonders is important. I share this with you to tell you that what you journal is no joke. It's sent from heaven to encourage you, to edify you, and to bring you into a deeper relationship with Jesus. Here are three things God has told me about fire that you can take into your future in this season. (I received these points after journalling.)

1. **You will fire on all cylinders in all areas of your life.** This means you'll get creative ideas and a sense of order and strategy.

2. **Your fire is your passion for Jesus, and as you journal, that fire will keep burning**. This means you'll have a stronger desire to be in God's presence.

3. **You will take the fire wherever you go,** and everything you are in contact with will be set on fire for God—your neighbourhood, your city, your nation, and the globe.

This means you'll actually make an impact for Jesus in the world around you.

Partnering with the Prophetic

1. Confess "I can do all things through Christ that strengthens me"

CHAPTER 10

YOUR SEASON FOR FRESH OIL

The lord will anoint you with fresh oil

Psalms 92:10

I was talking about God to my wife when my daughter turned to my wife and whispered a few times. I asked my wife what she said, and my wife said, "Tatiana said, 'When I grow up, I want to know God much more than daddy does.'" When I heard that, I felt the Holy Spirit say, "Anoint her and impart some of your gift to her," and I was led to Psalms 92:10.

I felt God tell me to put fresh oil on my child. If you are reading this, you understand that this is a season of fresh oil! A fresh anointing! All the dry places in your life are going to receive oil.

I turned to my daughter and said, "Because of what you desire, I'm going to anoint you." I got some oil, and I did! But here's the mystery. I have two daughters and my second born was watching her sister get anointed with oil. I could see that she was jealous. Have you ever been in a place where someone else looked blessed and prosperous, and you felt left out because you can't identify the blessing in your life? I could see that our second-born daughter felt that way while watching her sister getting anointed. My second born had Godly jealousy; she wanted a blessing too, and there's nothing wrong with wanting a blessing. Nothing at all.

Fresh oil

So, I reached for the same oil that I put on my firstborn and was about to anoint my second-born daughter with the same oil. As I walked toward her, the Holy Spirit said, "Malachi, use a different oil because what I am doing in your firstborn's life is different from what I am going to do in your second born's life."

God wants to give you fresh oil—an anointing that you've never received before and a different set of gifts, opportunities, blessings; things you've not experienced before, an ability that you've never operated before, something new, something ground-breaking. That's what fresh oil will bring into your life. A totally new flow of the spirit!

This is fresh oil

Just as a rusty door handle doesn't work properly until it's oiled, fresh oil will help you function better. When God anoints you with fresh oil, you'll have new ideas, the Holy Spirit will bring things back to your remembrance, and you'll have the desire to do new things. God will anoint the creative side of your brain, from where new ideas flow. Your creativity and productivity are going to rise like never before.

You'll get business ideas, health secrets, and songwriting secrets. I'm not sure what your anointing is, but it is going to grow, it's going to expand, and things are going to shift and change!

The key to experiencing fresh oil is to cry out for it.

PRAY THIS PRAYER

"Lord, please give me fresh oil. Touch me, Lord; help me to flow in new levels of creativity and productivity. Help me to see differently and flow on a whole new level, in Jesus' name. "

CHAPTER 11

AN OCTOBER OUTPOURING

**God will shower down His blessings
all over your life**

*"That ye may be the children of your Father which is
in heaven: for he maketh his sun to rise on the evil
and on the good, and sendeth rain on the just and on
the unjust."*

Matthew 5:45

For years, I didn't recognize this, but October was always a blessed time, especially when it came to opportunities. I would get either speaking engagements, invitations to host events, or a little bonus at work.

I didn't have spiritual terms to define this; in fact, I didn't even think this was spiritual until a few years ago when I discovered the rainy seasons of Israel.

When I received those prophetic words about **April showers,** and during my research about the rains, I discovered there were two rainy seasons in Israel, called the latter and former rain. But what I didn't know is that rain also falls in **October and November** (the former rain), and the spring rain falls in March and April (the latter rain). The latter rain, also called the "rain in the springtime" (Zec 10:1), is a timely rain because it is absolutely needed for a good harvest.

The former and latter rain, which comes at the right time for farming in Israel, is a blessing from God. So most of the rain recorded in the Bible figuratively represents God's grace and blessings (Eze 34:26).

The outpouring is God's choice

Knowing the seasons is so important! The Bible says in Psalms 1 that whatever you does in His season shall prosper. There are seasons in God, and October is a season of outpouring. I remember a friend phoning me to say, "Malachi, I have had so many testimonies this month. God has been good." I sat there laughing, knowing that he was experiencing an outpouring in

October. God is showering down his blessings because that's what He wants to do. It is so important to know that God wants to bless you so much that He has times and seasons when He pours out more than you can receive. God is simply that good. Expect this season to be one when God sends an outpouring of blessing because He is God, and the rain falls on the just and the unjust. In this case, God is pouring out the rain because HE WANTS TO.

Partnering with the Prophetic

1. This month, journal every good thing that happens to you. (Remember, this is a time of outpouring.)

CHAPTER 12

BY THIS TIME TOMORROW

Your blessing will come by this time tomorrow

Joshua 11:6

*T*his is one of the strangest journalling experiences I've had, but it left me encouraged with a new hunger for science. As I was journaling about a few things, I suddenly stopped after this phrase the Holy Spirit gave me: "You are a mushroom." I put my pen down; I was confused. I don't know anything about mushrooms, so it didn't really mean much to me. But I was curious, so I went and did some research.

I was fascinated with what I discovered about mushrooms.

I discovered that mushrooms grow best in dark, damp places. "Mushrooms can grow without light because they are not plants. A mushroom is only the fruiting body – that is, the reproductive structure – of a much-larger fungus body that grows unseen in rotting logs, rich humus, and dark, damp places." https://tinyurl.com/yckuybb7

I thought about the dark seasons in life—the winter seasons or even those when we are in the valley of the shadow of death. These places can be the perfect place for personal and spiritual growth. Isn't it wonderful how God sees our adversity? It helped me understand that growth isn't always beautiful and that sometimes adversity can help us become all that we can be for Christ.

I did some more research and what I discovered was amazing. "Many familiar mushrooms have fruiting bodies that are fleshy and umbrella-shaped. Warm, damp weather triggers their sudden appearance. Usually first to be noticed are small, round "button caps" composed of densely packed hyphae. Soon after, the outer covering ruptures, the stem elongates, and the cap enlarges to its full size. This entire process can indeed happen overnight!" https://tinyurl.com/yckuybb7

Mushrooms don't just grow in the dark; they grow rapidly and appear suddenly. This can happen within twenty-four hours! Due to the way that the cells of the mushroom are designed, they can suddenly appear fully grown within hours or overnight.

I went back to God and began to journal again. Here's what I received.

"Mushrooms grow suddenly; they grow overnight! Stop thinking that your growth will take a long time. You have a foundation. You have the experience. You have the cells to grow. Those cells will grow rapidly, and before you know it, you will reach the level I've called you to. Over the years, you've been creating the cells and manufacturing the compost. Now, at any time, boom! You'll be at the level and in the place I want you to be—in your job, in your health, and even in your finances.

Mushrooms grow in the dark, but they also grow quickly. This is why I called you a mushroom, for this is how it will be for you. It will look as if nothing is happening, and then suddenly things will appear. Don't always look at what you can see, for often a lot is happening when you can't see it.

Things will happen overnight. They will happen overnight! There are going to be some things that you don't understand and some that you WILL understand but you're not going to know how you understand them. There are going to be some things that you can just do, and you won't know how you learned to do them.

There will be some things that just happen and just appear, and you'll think they are strange, but all of these things have been growing underground, behind the scenes, and you are about to step into them. This is an overnight blessing; in My Word I call it "by this time tomorrow." Things can happen overnight!

The mushroom is a metaphor.

Just as mushrooms suddenly appear and grow overnight, answered prayers are going to suddenly appear, quickly. Yet they won't be premature but, rather, mature and fully developed. Just as the Holy Spirit came suddenly in Acts 2:2. Just as all of a sudden the prison doors were burst open in Acts 16:26. Just as the man suddenly came to Jesus and was healed in Matthew 8:2.

- *The right spouse*

- *That speaking engagement*

- *That role in a movie*

- *That promotion at work*

- *That job you've been looking for*

By this time tomorrow, these things can literally appear just as the mushroom does. The key is to realise that just because things can't be seen on the surface doesn't mean that nothing's happening underground. Get ready and expect things to happen out of nowhere."

Reflections by Mark Virkler

A couple of weeks ago, a lady in our online class was instantly healed of long standing neck pain while we were simply practising speaking a personalised Scripture verse over ourselves: "By His stripes, I (insert name) AM healed!" That is a "suddenly" move of God's power and grace.

A couple of days ago I held a beautiful Zoom counselling session where a dozen or so demons were cast out quite easily with a clear manifestation of release and peace accompanying the prayer time. That was wonderful to see—the ease and swiftness of the deliverance.

I am seeing "suddenlies" in my ministry and sense in my spirit that there are "suddenlies" ready to sweep the earth. So lift up your eyes, for your redemption draweth nigh! Celebrate the returning King, Who is coming to manifest His glory in a historic worldwide revival!

Partnering with the Prophetic

September -- November read *Deuteronomy 7:14 Matthew 3:11* **Psalms 92:10 Matthew 5:45,** Joshua 11:6

Confessions for this season

1. *Barrenness is broken in my life, and I will give birth*

2. *I am a fire starter*

3. *My blessing will show up by this time tomorrow*

4. *The Lord has anointed me with fresh oil*

5. *God will shower down his blessings all over my life*

END-OF-SEASON TESTIMONY

What did God do for you in this season?

....

....

....

....

....

....

....

....

....

....

....

....

....

....

....

....

....

....

....

END-OF-SEASON TESTIMONY

What blessings or breakthroughs did you experience?

A NOTE FROM THE AUTHOR

I pray that these words are a blessing to you and that they encourage you. Pray about them and expect God to move on your behalf.

Journalling and talking to God like He is your friend is probably the best thing you can do to build the intimacy levels in your relationship with God. I've been journaling with Jesus for over twenty years, and what started as a few scribbles on a piece of paper has turned into books, courses, and words for the season. I didn't know that this would happen. I've just been faithful to journalling and listening for God's voice. I thank God for His grace and that He does speak to us. From this day onward, commit to journalling, ask God what He is doing in a season, talk to Him about His plans for you, and watch your spiritual life go to the next level. See yourself make decisions that benefit your children's children.

We hope you enjoyed this book, here are some more resources from Malachi Talabi

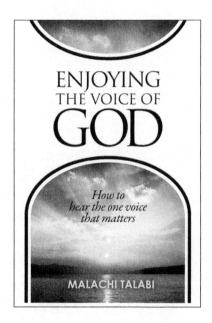

Latest book from
MALACHI TALABI

EDIFIED
Build Yourself Up

Unlock mysteries
and transform
your life with this
neglected
prayer tool.

Paperback -
by Malachi Talabi (Author)

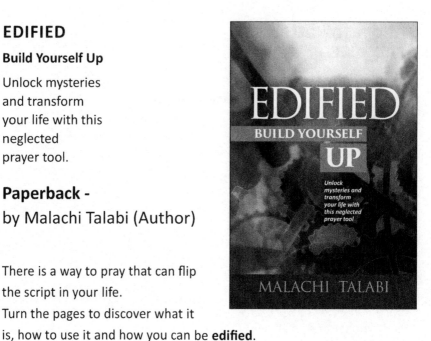

There is a way to pray that can flip
the script in your life.
Turn the pages to discover what it
is, how to use it and how you can be **edified**.

The principles in edified will help you step into

- Better decision-making
- Increased anointing
- Spiritual victory
- Personal transformation
- Increased intimacy with God

Latest book from
MALACHI TALABI

JOURNALING WITH JESUS

How to hear God's voice through the sacred art of journaling

Paperback -
by Malachi Talabi (Author)

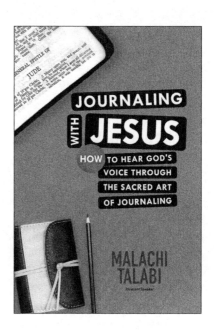

God wants to speak to us, and when we journal, we show Him that what He has to say is important!

This book will teach you:

- What journaling with Jesus is
- How to see in the spirit—debunked, debugged and without an ounce of confusion
- How to be still without being frustrated or bored, or falling asleep
- 4 keys to hearing God's voice
- How to hear God clearly– so that you can avoid the mistakes and pitfalls that I experienced on my
- Journaling with Jesus journey

Availble at
www.malachitalabiministries.com

Latest book from
MALACHI TALABI

SPRITUAL GIFTS UNWRAPPED

Know, grow and flow in the gifts of the Holy Spirit

Paperback -
by Malachi Talabi (Author)

It's time to unwrap spiritual gifts and learn how they function. If you have dreamed of being used by God, or you simply want a deeper understanding of spiritual gifts, then you will enjoy this book.

Prepare for an adventure because after reading this you will:

- Understand all of the nine gifts of the Spirit, inside out
- Operate in spiritual gifts
- Have the confidence that God is using you
- Learn how to work with how you are wired
- Discover how to get solutions from heaven

Go and get your pen, highlighter, and notebook as we unwrap spiritual gifts.

Availble at
www.malachitalabiministries.com